Understanding the
COVID-19 Pandemic

The Origins and
SPREAD OF COVID-19

John Allen

ReferencePoint
Press

San Diego, CA

About the Author

John Allen is a writer who lives in Oklahoma City.

For more information, contact:
ReferencePoint Press, Inc.
PO Box 27779
San Diego, CA 92198
www.ReferencePointPress.com

Picture Credits:
Cover: Olga Kashubin/Shutterstock
 9: Maury Aaseng
12: Chirag Nagpal/Shutterstock
16: AhXiong/Shutterstock
21: SplashNews/Newscom
23: vladeva/Shutterstock
26: Associated Press

31: Morteza Nikoubazl/Zuma Press/Newscom
35: Chine Nouvelle/Sipa/Newscom
38: Associated Press
43: Alexanderstock23/Shutterstock
47: Micha Weber/Shutterstock
48: nyker/Shutterstock.com
51: Larry Marano/SplashNews/Newscom

LIBRARY OF CONGRESS CATALOGING-IN-PUBLICATION DATA

Names: Allen, John, 1957- author.
Title: The origins and spread of COVID-19 / by John Allen.
Description: San Diego : ReferencePoint Press, Inc., 2021. | Series:
   Understanding the COVID-19 pandemic | Includes bibliographical
   references and index.
Identifiers: LCCN 2020043274 (print) | LCCN 2020043275 (ebook) | ISBN
   9781678200381 (library binding) | ISBN 9781678200398 (ebook)
Subjects: LCSH: COVID-19 (Disease)--Juvenile literature. | COVID-19
   (Disease)--China--Wuhan--Juvenile literature. | Epidemics--Juvenile
   literature.
Classification: LCC RA644.C67 A634 2021 (print) | LCC RA644.C67 (ebook) |
   DDC 614.5/92414--dc23
LC record available at https://lccn.loc.gov/2020043274
LC ebook record available at https://lccn.loc.gov/2020043275

CONTENTS

The COVID-19 Pandemic:
The First Nine Months of 2020

January

(11) China reports first known death from mysterious virus that infected dozens in Wuhan in December.

(20) WHO reports that Japan, South Korea, and Thailand have first confirmed virus cases outside of mainland China.

(30) WHO declares global health emergency.

(31) US restricts travel from China.

February

(2) Philippines reports first coronavirus death outside of China.

(5) Japan quarantines *Diamond Princess* cruise ship; within 2 weeks the ship has more than 600 infections.

(11) WHO names the disease caused by the new coronavirus COVID-19 (for *corona*virus *d*isease 20*19*).

(23) Europe's first major outbreak occurs in Italy.

(26) Brazil has Latin America's first known case of coronavirus.

March

(13) US president Donald Trump officially declares national emergency.

(19) California becomes first US state to enact statewide shutdown.

(24) Officials announce 1-year postponement of 2020 Tokyo Summer Olympics.

(26) US becomes world leader in confirmed coronavirus infections.

(27) President Trump signs $2 trillion economic stimulus bill sent to him by Congress.

April

(2) Pandemic shutdowns have cost nearly 10 million Americans their jobs.

(10) Coronavirus cases surge in Russia.

(14) IMF warns of worst global downturn since Great Depression.

(17) President Trump encourages protests of social distancing restrictions.

(26) Pandemic has killed more than 200,000 and sickened more than 2.8 million worldwide.

(30) Several major airlines begin requiring face masks.

May

1 FDA authorizes remdesivir as an emergency treatment for COVID-19.

17 Japan and Germany fall into recession.

26 Widespread protests begin after George Floyd is killed by Minneapolis police; because many protesters wear masks, feared virus outbreaks do not occur.

27 US has more than 100,000 COVID-19 deaths, surpassing all other nations.

June

4 Previously spared regions of Middle East, Latin America, Africa, and South Asia have large spikes.

11 Coronavirus cases in Africa exceed 200,000, with one-fourth in South Africa.

20 Florida and South Carolina are among 19 US states experiencing sharp rise in new infections.

28 Final phase of clinical trials for AstraZeneca–University of Oxford COVID-19 vaccine begins in Brazil.

July

11 For the first time, President Trump wears a mask during a public appearance.

16 Georgia's governor rescinds local government mask mandates.

17 After easing restrictions in May, skyrocketing infections force India to reimpose lockdown.

27 Final phase of clinical trials for Moderna COVID-19 vaccine begins in the US.

August

9 New Zealand achieves 100 days without a new diagnosis of coronavirus.

11 Amid global skepticism, Russia announces first approved-for-use coronavirus vaccine.

17 Democrats begin first-ever, all-virtual convention to nominate the party's presidential candidate, Joe Biden.

23 FDA authorizes convalescent plasma as an emergency treatment for COVID-19.

27 Before a crowd of about 1,500 people, President Trump accepts Republican presidential nomination.

September

8 Nine of the leading drug companies developing COVID-19 vaccines pledge in writing to put safety before speed.

21 President Trump tells supporters at an Ohio rally that COVID "affects virtually nobody."

30 The pandemic has killed more than 1 million people and sickened nearly 34 million worldwide. In the US, the pandemic has killed nearly 207,000 people and sickened more than 7 million. Two days later, on October 2, President Trump tweets that he and First Lady Melania Trump have tested positive for the virus that causes COVID-19.

Based on Derrick Bryson Taylor, "A Timeline of the Coronavirus Pandemic," *New York Times*, July 21, 2020. www.nytimes.com.

A World-Changing Virus

On March 11, 2020, the professional basketball game between the hometown Oklahoma City Thunder and the visiting Utah Jazz was moments away from tip-off when chaos erupted. As the players prepared to take the court, the Thunder's team doctor suddenly dashed from the locker room with an urgent message for the referees. Jazz center Rudy Gobert (who was back at his team's hotel) had tested positive for COVID-19, a deadly and contagious new virus. Minutes later the officials directed both teams to leave the floor. The public address announcer explained that the game was postponed due to unforeseen circumstances.

The fallout was swift and devastating. Within hours the National Basketball Association suspended all its games until further notice. Other sports leagues and entertainment venues in the United States quickly followed suit. The cancellations were early signs of how the spread of COVID-19 would upend daily life in the United States as it already had around the world. From its murky origins in China to its rapid development into a full-blown health crisis, the disease has killed hundreds of thousands worldwide and led government leaders to lock down their economies and quarantine their citizens. According to Dr. Anthony Fauci, director of the National Institute of Allergy and Infectious Diseases, "It really is the perfect storm and [an] infectious disease and public health person's worst nightmare."[1]

A Mysterious New Disease

Reports about the mysterious and potentially deadly new disease first began to appear in late December 2019. COVID-19 is caused by a novel coronavirus, meaning a new virus that has not previously been identified in humans. The virus appears to have originated in Wuhan, the largest city of Hubei Province in central China. On February 11, 2020, the World Health Organization (WHO) gave the disease its official name. *COVID-19* means a *coronavirus disease discovered in 2019*. One month later, on March 11, 2020, the WHO declared the disease a pandemic—meaning the number of cases rapidly increased across a wide area, in this instance throughout the globe. WHO director-general Tedros Adhanom Ghebreyesus noted the alarming spread of COVID-19 and the equally alarming lack of urgency in addressing its threat. By that time health officials had already identified 118,000 cases in 114 countries, with 4,291 reported deaths.

COVID-19 is especially dangerous because it is a new disease. Unlike the seasonal flu, there is currently no vaccine to protect people from infection. Also, it has proved to be easy to transmit from one person to another. It is thought to spread mostly via respiratory droplets from coughing, sneezing, or talking. It can also spread by contact with infected surfaces, such as doorknobs, countertops, and subway railings, although this seems to occur less often than by human contact. In the early days of the virus's outbreak, health officials stressed certain habits to avoid infection. These included washing hands or using hand sanitizer frequently, keeping several feet away from others in public, and wearing a mask to cover the mouth and nose.

> "It really is the perfect storm and [an] infectious disease and public health person's worst nightmare."[1]
>
> —Dr. Anthony Fauci, director of the National Institute of Allergy and Infectious Diseases

The novel coronavirus varies widely in its effects on people. Some, especially adolescents and young adults, become infected yet show no symptoms of disease, although they can still spread the virus. Others can experience severe infections in their lungs and respiratory systems, making it difficult to breathe. The body's immune system reacts with a flood of antibodies that unexpectedly worsens the victim's condition. Such severe infections often are fatal, especially for the elderly and people with serious underlying health conditions. As COVID-19 has spread in the United States, statistics show that people of color are more likely to face dire consequences from the disease.

Slowing the Spread

Health experts have long warned of potential disaster from a deadly virus spreading rapidly in global populations. In the past century there have been three major outbreaks of influenza, in 1918, 1957, and 1968. The 1918 outbreak, an H1N1 flu virus called the Spanish flu, was the worst, with an estimated 50 million deaths worldwide and 675,000 in the United States alone. With international travel much more frequent today, COVID-19 presents an even greater threat to global health than these past pandemics.

In nations around the world, government leaders and health officials have employed various strategies to slow the spread of COVID-19. Their methods have ranged from tight controls to more relaxed guidelines and have been met with varied levels of success. China's ruling Communist Party claims to have crushed the virus through forced lockdowns in Wuhan and travel restrictions inside the country. Japan, by contrast, had success limiting the virus's spread without large-scale shutdowns. Sweden kept schools and businesses open, resulting in a death rate that initially was much higher than neighboring countries but later fell rapidly. The response in the United States has been a patchwork that varies from state to state, despite calls for the federal government to pursue an overall national plan. The United States has sustained the world's highest number of cases and deaths from COVID-19.

Researchers in the United States and elsewhere have urgently pursued vaccines and treatments that could bring an end to the COVID pandemic. Widespread use of an effective vaccine could help limit transmission of the virus. Meanwhile, many nations have

The United States Leads the World in COVID-19 Deaths

The United States is the world leader in COVID-19 deaths. As of September 30, 2020, the United States had 207,000 confirmed deaths from COVID-19, according to data compiled by the Coronavirus Resource Center at Johns Hopkins University. Brazil, with 147,494 COVID-19 deaths, was the number two nation, followed by India, with 104,555 deaths. The Johns Hopkins University site uses data from numerous sources and updates the numbers multiple times each day.

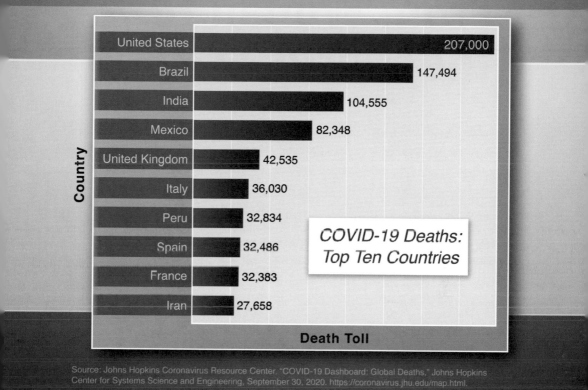

COVID-19 Deaths: Top Ten Countries

Country	Death Toll
United States	207,000
Brazil	147,494
India	104,555
Mexico	82,348
United Kingdom	42,535
Italy	36,030
Peru	32,834
Spain	32,486
France	32,383
Iran	27,658

Source: Johns Hopkins Coronavirus Resource Center, "COVID-19 Dashboard: Global Deaths," Johns Hopkins Center for Systems Science and Engineering, September 30, 2020. https://coronavirus.jhu.edu/map.html.

experienced disastrous effects from the pandemic and from efforts to contain it, including economic collapse, social unrest, and emotional turmoil. These impacts—as well as the more obvious health dangers—have strained the well-being of families and individuals. "Because it's everywhere, because it hits us 24/7, we tend to lose track of the effects of COVID on our daily lives, mood and consciousness," says Edwin Fisher, a professor of health behavior at the Gillings School of Global Public Health at the University of North Carolina. "Well, what will the similar effect be of having lived through the greatest global pandemic in over 100 years? There are going to be many, many long-term effects."[2]

CHAPTER ONE

From Wuhan to the World

On December 30, 2019, Li Wenliang delivered an urgent message to a group of his fellow doctors via an online chat room. Li, a thirty-four-year-old eye doctor at Wuhan Central Hospital, warned that he had seen several cases of a virus that resembled SARS, a severe respiratory illness that had spread worldwide in 2003. Li urged his friends to wear special clothing and gear to protect themselves from infection. What Li did not yet know was that the virus was something new—and deadly.

Li's comments quickly reached government security officials. At the time, the Chinese Communist Party (CCP) claimed the virus was transmitted only by contact with animals. There were no safety guidelines yet for doctors. On January 1, 2020, the Wuhan Public Security Bureau accused Li, along with seven others, of spreading false rumors and disturbing the social order. Officials forced him to sign a public letter admitting to his supposed offense. One week later, while treating a patient, Li caught the virus himself. In a blog post, Li described how he began coughing, developed a fever a day later, then had to be hospitalized. He died on February 6, 2020. Li's death brought a flood of emotional posts from his followers. One person feared what Li's story—the attempt to silence his truth telling—would mean for China and the world. "Dr Li Wenliang is a hero," this person wrote. "In the future, doctors will be more afraid to issue early warnings when they find signs of infectious diseases. A safer public health environment . . . requires tens of millions of Li Wenliang."[3]

Delays and Frustration

The first documented cases of the mysterious disease had been diagnosed in Wuhan in early December 2019. This was almost a month before Li noticed the virus. Experts believe cases may have arisen as early as two months prior. What is certain is that by January 2, 2020, the Wuhan Institute of Virology, with incredible speed, had mapped the virus's genome, or genetic code. This information was vital to beginning research on the virus worldwide. Yet China delayed sharing the genetic map for more than a week, preferring to let three Chinese government labs work on evaluating the data first.

On January 7, Xi Jinping, China's president and head of the CCP, took control of the nation's response to the virus. Two days later authorities finally admitted that the viral outbreak in Wuhan was due to a novel coronavirus, similar to SARS. Details about how infectious the disease appeared to be were still withheld. It was not until January 11, when one lab published the genome on a virology website, that the Chinese government authorized public release of the genetic data. Moreover, China waited another two weeks to provide the WHO with details about cases, patients, and symptoms. At this early stage, according to health experts, sharing information could have slowed the outbreak to a significant degree.

The delays frustrated officials at the WHO. "We're going on very minimal information," said American epidemiologist Maria Van Kerkhove in a meeting with WHO colleagues. "It's clearly not enough for you to do proper planning."[4] United Nations member

"Dr Li Wenliang is a hero. In the future, doctors will be more afraid to issue early warnings when they find signs of infectious diseases. A safer public health environment . . . requires tens of millions of Li Wenliang."[3]

—A Chinese commenter posting online

A nurse in a protective suit feeds a novel coronavirus patient inside an isolated ward at Zhongnan Hospital of Wuhan University in China on February 8, 2020. The first documented case of the disease was diagnosed in Wuhan in early December 2019.

countries are required to share vital health information at once with the WHO, although the UN agency has no way to force compliance.

Chinese officials fumbled or suppressed information about the coronavirus in other ways. In December 2019 test results from several labs in Wuhan showed that viral pneumonia patients in the city had contracted the same infectious disease. Yet officials and medical workers kept their concerns to themselves. According to the *Straits Times* of Singapore, an official at the Hubei Provincial Health Commission contacted one genetics-testing company and ordered it to stop testing samples of the Wuhan virus. The company was also told to stop releasing test results and to destroy all remaining samples. Government orders prevented information about the virus from being shared much earlier.

Internally, the Chinese Center for Disease Control and Prevention (China CDC) labeled the coronavirus a level one emergency, the most serious rating. Yet on January 15 Li Qun, head of the China CDC's emergency center, told Chinese state television that the risk of human-to-human spread was low. Li's statement directly contradicted what dozens of Wuhan doctors, medical workers, and lab technicians already knew: the novel coronavirus was highly transmissible from person to person and likely to spread rapidly. "We knew then that the government was lying," says one local doctor in Wuhan. "But we don't know why they needed to lie. Maybe they thought it could be controlled."[5] In the race to unlock the virus's secrets, such delays and deceptions would prove crucial.

> "We knew then that the government was lying. But we don't know why they needed to lie. Maybe they thought [the coronavirus] could be controlled."[5]
>
> —A local doctor in Wuhan

A Fateful Celebration

One week after the China CDC's announcement, Xi and the CCP reversed course. Xi seemed to realize that his nation's credibility worldwide was at stake. As a result, Chinese authorities admitted that the novel coronavirus was a major threat to the population. The *People's Daily*, the CCP's official newspaper, detailed how Xi was marshaling all available resources to fight the outbreak. Officially, the government began to call for complete openness regarding information. As the nation's main law enforcement commission warned, "Anyone who deliberately delays and hides the reporting of [virus] cases out of his or her own self-interest will be nailed on the pillar of shame for eternity."[6]

Nonetheless, Wuhan was not only ground zero for the coronavirus. This huge city of 11 million people, 3 million more than New York City, was also host of an annual gathering of legislators and advisory groups. As usual, local authorities were anxious to present their city in the best possible light by concealing bad news.

No new cases of the coronavirus were reported from January 6 to 17. And, in a fateful decision doubtlessly approved by Xi, the city went ahead with its traditional celebration of Chinese Lunar New Year beginning on January 18.

The festivities presented ideal conditions for spreading the virus. Forty thousand families attended an enormous potluck banquet in Wuhan. During the event, people embraced old friends, crowded together to take photos, and shared home-cooked dishes with chopsticks. Afterward, many of the attendees, part of a flood of some 5 million people allowed to leave Wuhan, jetted off to destinations around the world. There was no preflight screening of passengers for the coronavirus. In one community in Hubei Province, fifty-seven residential centers were designated as "fever buildings" after residents who had attended the banquet became ill.

On January 21 Wuhan mayor Zhou Xianwang revealed in an interview that Hubei had 270 confirmed cases and that six Wuhan citizens had died after becoming infected. Already the first cases and deaths were being reported outside China, in Japan, South Korea, and Thailand. With Wuhan the epicenter of the viral outbreak, many experts say Chinese officials missed the chance to limit the global spread of COVID-19. In March 2020 a research report from data experts at the United Kingdom's University of Southampton found that "if interventions in the country could have been conducted one week, two weeks, or three weeks earlier, cases could have been reduced by 66 percent, 86 percent and 95 percent respectively—significantly limiting the geographical spread of the disease."[7] China has rejected criticism of its reaction, claiming to have acted swiftly and responsibly.

Speculation About the Virus's Origin

As medical experts around the world became aware of the novel coronavirus, they speculated about how it first arose in humans. They believed details on its origin could hold clues about how to fight it. Researchers in China noted how several of the first docu-

Coronavirus and the Virus Lab in Wuhan

Scientists overwhelmingly agree that the coronavirus that causes COVID-19 emerged from an animal, probably a bat. Some skeptics have challenged the scientific consensus, speculating that the coronavirus escaped from a Wuhan research laboratory. They note that as the virus was spreading in January 2020, China's military sent its top epidemiologist to the Wuhan Institute of Virology. And in February President Xi demanded stronger biosafety rules to control viruses in laboratory settings. The skeptics see these clues as a possible connection between the coronavirus and the Institute of Virology.

The deputy director of the institute scoffed at the idea that the virus came from her laboratory. Shi Zhengli, called the "bat woman" for her work with viruses in bats, insisted that she first encountered the novel coronavirus in December 2019 and that she and her colleagues had never seen it before.

On September 14, 2020, Li-Meng Yan, a Chinese virologist in Hong Kong, posted online that the coronavirus was human-made in a Chinese lab. Yan claimed she got her information from local doctors working with the China CDC. "The market in Wuhan . . . is a smoke screen and this virus is not from nature," she says. For now, the real origin of the coronavirus remains a mystery.

Quoted in Tamar Lapin, "Chinese Virologist Posts Report Claiming COVID-19 Was Made in Wuhan Lab," *New York Post*, September 14, 2020. www.nypost.com.

mented cases were linked to the Huanan Seafood Wholesale Market. This was a so-called wet market in Wuhan where seafood, animals, and birds were sold. The market featured a variety of exotic wildlife, with animals in cages and carcasses hung in the open air for buyers' inspection. Everything from beavers and porcupines to snakes and baby crocodiles could be purchased there.

Among the first cases of coronavirus in Wuhan was a fifty-seven-year-old seafood vendor at the Huanan market named Wei Guixian. On December 10, 2019, Wei felt ill with fever and walked to a small clinic nearby for treatment. Within eight days she was

Several of the first documented cases of the novel coronavirus were linked to the Huanan Seafood Wholesale Market, which is similar to this wet market in Singapore. The government shut down the Huanan wet market on January 1, 2020.

lying half-conscious in a hospital bed struggling to breathe. By late December doctors at several hospitals had exchanged information linking Wei and several other cases of the strange new pneumonia to the Huanan market. They quarantined her and other coronavirus patients while delivering warnings to hospital managers. Authorities forbid these doctors to alert their colleagues or the public about the threat posed by the virus. The truth emerged only when Li Wenliang and a few others shared reports on social media. Once connections to the Huanan market were established, the government shut down the market on January 1, 2020. Wei recovered fully and spent the next two months locked down in her apartment.

Researchers at first believed that the COVID-19 virus passed from an animal, such as a bat, to a human at the market. Some suggested that another animal, perhaps a pangolin (a scaly anteater), may have been involved in the early transmission. Other viruses, such as SARS, have sprung from human contact with horseshoe bats. In fact, two major facilities that investigate how viruses emerge from wildlife are located in Wuhan, one of them only 300 yards (274 m) from the Huanan market.

Further study, however, convinced researchers that animals at the Huanan market were not the source of the novel coronavirus. Tests on animals sold at the market showed no trace of the virus that led to COVID-19. Scientists believe the virus was instead lurking on surfaces at the market and spread that way. "None of the animals [at Huanan] tested positive," says Colin Carlson, a professor at Georgetown University who studies viruses that go from animals to humans. "This is an animal-origin virus that made the leap, maybe from bats to humans, maybe through . . . another animal, maybe through livestock. And we don't have the data yet to know where or how. That takes time."[8] Carlson notes that the definitive study showing that SARS came from bats appeared in 2017, fifteen years after the first outbreak of SARS.

Locking Down to Stop the Spread

By late January Chinese health officials realized the novel coronavirus represented an even greater threat than SARS or other similar viruses. The situation called for drastic measures. Although visitors to Wuhan for the Lunar New Year had been allowed to leave the country, travel within China was now severely restricted. In addition, a task force led by Zhong Nanshan, one of China's leading epidemiologists, recommended a tactic to stop the virus that had rarely been used in modern times. On January 23, Xi and CCP officials ordered a complete lockdown of Wuhan and three other cities in Hubei Province. Under the quarantine, more than 20 million people had to remain indoors until further notice.

People were not allowed to leave or enter the locked-down cities, and many businesses were closed to customers.

As the lockdowns took effect, the normally bustling streets of Wuhan stood eerily empty in broad daylight. No one could predict the effects of such stringent measures on a large population. Getting food, medicine, and household supplies proved to be a challenge. Staple foods such as rice and noodles sold out immediately. Face masks and sanitizing liquids became nearly impossible to obtain. "I went to a pharmacy and it was already limiting the number of shoppers," wrote Guo Jing, a twenty-nine-year-old social worker, in her diary. "It had already sold out of masks and alcohol disinfectant. . . . After going home, I washed all my clothes and took a shower. Personal hygiene is important—I think I am washing my hands 20 to 30 times a day."[9]

"I went to a pharmacy and it was already limiting the number of shoppers. It had already sold out of masks and alcohol disinfectant. . . . After going home, I washed all my clothes and took a shower."[9]

—Guo Jing, a twenty-nine-year-old social worker in Wuhan

Many Wuhan residents turned to internet delivery services such as the online giant Tencent. Ordering apps were adapted so that delivery workers could leave food packages outside and customers could avoid face-to-face meetings. Neighbors checked on elderly residents living alone to see that they had sufficient stocks. Overworked hospital medical staff received thousands of free meals from delivery services, along with fresh vegetables for occasional meals at home.

With patient counts and deaths from the virus rising rapidly, Wuhan chat rooms were buzzing with worry. Many infected patients had to be turned away from hospitals due to lack of beds. Small regional hospitals were not equipped to handle the onrush of the seriously ill. However, in the ensuing five weeks, the lockdown helped slow the spread of the coronavirus. A research team at the University of Pennsylvania affirmed the lockdown's success. According to the team's estimates, cases of COVID-19 in more than three hundred

Trusting China's Numbers

On April 17, 2020, the city of Wuhan revised its official coronavirus death toll by 50 percent, adding 1,290 to the total. This raised the overall death numbers in China to more than 3,800. Yet US intelligence agencies advised the White House that even these numbers could not be trusted. Sources inside China insisted that the CCP was underreporting COVID-19 deaths by a wide margin.

Part of the problem was that local and regional party bosses feared reprimands from their superiors if the number of reported deaths was too high. Changes in official tallies created a great deal of confusion about the extent of the crisis in China. And it came at a time when the rest of the world desperately needed information about the severity of COVID-19.

By September 2020 China had reported only about forty-five hundred total deaths from COVID-19—a tiny fraction of the death tolls in the United States, Brazil, and many European nations. Whether the Chinese numbers can be believed is another matter. As noted by Adam Kamradt-Scott, associate professor of global health security at the University of Sydney in Australia, "There's still ongoing concerns about the level of transparency around the data from China."

Quoted in Charlie Campbell and Amy Gunia, "China Says It's Beating Coronavirus. But Can We Believe Its Numbers?," *Time*, April 1, 2020. www.time.com.

Chinese cities outside Hubei Province would have been 65 percent higher without the Wuhan lockdown. In Hubei itself, cases outside Wuhan would have been 53 percent higher, the researchers claimed.

Hanming Fang, a professor of economics and health care who led the study, noted that the lockdown was unprecedented but seemed to be working. "The key thing it did was prevent a panicked outflow of people, some of them infected, to other cities," says Fang. "That early isolation of Wuhan slowed the spread of the disease by providing other cities with more time to prepare for their own wave of infections and patient loads."[10] Nonetheless, China struggled from the start to identify new cases, mainly due to a lack of testing kits. Later research, published in the science journal *Nature*, suggested that 87 percent of cases in Wuhan from January 1 to March 8 may have gone undetected, allowing for widespread transmission of the virus.

A Global Health Emergency

Experts at the WHO did not gain access to Wuhan until late January. On January 28 a WHO delegation led by Director-General Tedros Adhanom Ghebreyesus met with President Xi in Beijing. Delays in gaining information and access did not prevent Tedros from praising Xi and CCP officials for their swiftness and openness in confronting the virus. On January 30, with Wuhan in full lockdown, the WHO declared COVID-19 a global health emergency. It reported 7,818 cases overall, with all but 82 of these in China. Meanwhile, details about the coronavirus were beginning to emerge. It spread easily from person to person via droplets and aerosols from coughing, sneezing, or speaking. The elderly and those with preconditions such as diabetes or heart disease seemed to be at higher risk of serious illness, hospitalization, and death. Doctors and hospital workers faced constant danger of infection from treating patients flush with the virus.

The coronavirus had reached all thirty-one Chinese provinces and was feared to be spreading rapidly outside the country. Many nations banned travel to and from China. On January 31 the United States announced a ban on most travelers who had been in China in the past fourteen days. On February 2 a forty-four-year-old native of Wuhan died from COVID-19 in the Philippines, becoming the first known victim of the disease outside China. One month later, ninety-six countries and territories had imposed some form of travel restrictions to and from China. At that time, the WHO still advised against such restrictions, saying they generally failed to limit the spread of cases.

Wuhan officials finally ended the lockdown there on April 8, seventy-six days after it was imposed. Even after it was lifted, life in Wuhan did not return to normal. Residents remained wary of the virus, and business owners and workers alike were shell-shocked from the plunge in economic activity. Nonetheless, CCP officials touted the nation's success at taming the virus. They claimed that the number of new cases had plummeted and that only about thirty-two hundred Chinese people had died from COVID. As the coronavirus raged elsewhere in the world and death tolls mounted, many people had reason to doubt the truth of those figures.

From its murky origins in the vicinity of a Wuhan seafood market, the novel coronavirus that causes COVID-19 has become a scourge to nations around the world. While doctors such as Li Wenliang tried to deliver warnings about the virus early on, Chinese party officials sought to suppress the true story. Chinese scientists mapped the genome of the virus and shared this vital information with the world, but the government's failure to share information promptly and limit travel from Wuhan enabled the virus to escape China's borders and endanger world populations. The result has been the deadliest pandemic in more than a century.

CHAPTER TWO

Growing Alarm as the Virus Spreads

For passengers and crew of the *Diamond Princess*, what began as a pleasure cruise through Southeast Asia was turning into a nightmare. On February 3 the large ship docked in Yokohama, Japan, where it was greeted by ambulances and the flashing lights of emergency vehicles. Japanese medics in sky-blue gowns, masks, and visors fanned out on board to test passengers for the virus and conduct interviews to trace the spread. At least 9 of the ship's 2,666 guests and 1 of its 1,045 crew members had already contracted the coronavirus, apparently from an eighty-year-old passenger with a severe cough. The man had left the ship a week earlier in Hong Kong, where he was later diagnosed with COVID-19. In the closed environment of a cruise ship, with passengers and crew in constant contact, the virus seemed certain to spread rapidly. And with so many of the passengers being elderly and in danger from serious complications, the situation looked dire. "Anybody would be scared for their life, because day by day more and more people were getting infected," reported one crew member. "And we knew people were dying."[11] The plight of the *Diamond Princess* drew keen interest worldwide. People fretted that their own communities would be next to experience a deadly outbreak.

A Ship in Quarantine

To head off a wider health crisis, Japanese officials quarantined the ship, keeping passengers confined to their cabins.

Those who became ill were transported to local hospitals with extra safety precautions. Ultimately, nearly seven hundred of the passengers and crew aboard the *Diamond Princess* tested positive for COVID-19. At the time it was the largest outbreak outside China. Local residents expressed alarm at having the infected ship in their midst. "I live in Yokohama and seeing this happening so close frightened me," says Fumio Takenaka, a homemaker in a nearby district.

On Monday morning, first thing, I went to the shops and bought two big boxes of face masks and the largest bottle of hand sanitizing liquid I could find. I have to go shopping, my daughter has to go to school and my husband takes the train and is constantly meeting people at work. A couple of weeks ago, no one had even heard of the coronavirus, but now it's killing people and it's here in Yokohama. I don't want to take any chances.[12]

In February 2020 Japanese officials quarantined the Diamond Princess *(pictured on an earlier cruise) due to an outbreak of COVID-19 on the ship. Ultimately, nearly seven hundred of the passengers and crew aboard tested positive for COVID-19.*

By late February 2020 it was obvious that COVID-19 was even more lethal than other recent respiratory illnesses like SARS and MERS. More than 843,000 infections had already been reported worldwide, with at least 2,800 deaths. Fear and uncertainty were spreading faster than the virus. With the *Diamond Princess* in mind, authorities in Thailand refused to allow a cruise ship to dock in Bangkok— this despite no evidence of any infections on board. Thousands of tourists and business travelers canceled scheduled trips to Singapore, Thailand, South Korea, and other Asian locales. As fears about COVID-19 mounted, governments across Asia and the South Pacific scrambled to calm their citizens. Southeast Asian nations that depend on Chinese trade and investment for their lifeblood—such as Laos, Myanmar, and Indonesia—tended to downplay the threat in public statements. Visitors from China rarely were tested or quarantined in these nations. This led health experts to question official reports of very few coronavirus cases across the region.

A Deadly Outbreak in Italy

By late February 2020, COVID-19 had made its way to Europe. The European Union's policy of open borders, designed to spur trade and tourism, threatened to accelerate the spread of the coronavirus. As outbreaks arose on the Continent, Italy soon became one of the epicenters of new infections. The health care crisis that developed there, and the lessons learned from the government's response to the pandemic, would influence COVID-19 policies worldwide.

Italy's first death from COVID-19 was on February 21, although health officials believe the virus arrived there long before the first cases were reported and was mistaken for ordinary influenza. "The virus had probably been circulating for quite some time," says Flavia Riccardo, a researcher in the Department of Infectious Diseases at the Italian National Institute of Health. "This happened right when we were having our peak of influenza and people were presenting with influenza symptoms. . . . [The coronavirus] started unnoticed which means by the time we realized it, there were a lot of transmission chains happening."[13] On February 23 the Italian government declared a quarantine for twelve towns in Lombardy, a wealthy northwestern region known for its finance and fashion. These towns, with a total population of about fifty thousand, had reported the most recent cases of COVID-19. The

The *Diamond Princess* as a Test Case

The *Diamond Princess*, a cruise ship placed under quarantine in the port of Yokohama, inadvertently provided an ideal test case for the novel coronavirus. The ship's closed environment allowed the coronavirus to spread freely, giving medical experts a rare chance to study the nature of its threat. "Cruise ships are like an ideal experiment of a closed population," says John Ioannidis, an epidemiologist at Stanford University. "You know exactly who is there and at risk and you can measure everyone."

Researchers found that more than seven hundred on board caught the coronavirus in the month after quarantine was imposed. Only nine of the seven hundred died—a rate of 0.01—indicating to Ioannidis that the virus's fatality rate was probably much lower than early predictions. Japanese health officials made more than three thousand tests on board the ship. They began with elderly passengers and those who showed symptoms, but they also tested many with no symptoms. Of those infected aboard the ship, 18 percent had no symptoms. This showed the importance of looking for asymptomatic transmission. Results of the *Diamond Princess* study may not be applicable to whole countries and lockdown policies, but they have provided useful guidance for health officials.

Quoted in Smriti Mallapaty, "What the Cruise-Ship Outbreaks Reveal About COVID-19," *Nature*, March 26, 2020. www.nature.com.

government shut down schools, museums, and theaters and discouraged large gatherings. Despite the closures, most Italians still did not consider the coronavirus a serious threat. They viewed it as China's problem, too distant to affect their own lives.

Lockdowns and Complicating Factors

News across Italy was growing more alarming by the day. Hospitals and clinics in the Northwest were beginning to fill with seriously ill patients. On March 8 Prime Minister Giuseppe Conte announced a lockdown for all of Lombardy, as well as sixteen adjoining provinces. When reports about the lockdown leaked ahead of time, Italians by the thousands fled to the South to avoid the quarantine. This likely helped the virus spread even more rapidly. Two days later Conte locked down the entire country. The quarantine, unprecedented in modern Europe, affected more than 60 million people. Only essential businesses such as supermarkets and pharmacies could remain open. Nationwide, curfews were set at 6 p.m., and travel between cities without a permit was subject to a stiff fine.

Yet the strong measures failed to halt the relentless spread. Several factors worked to undermine Italy's quarantine policy.

People line up outside a supermarket in Turin, Italy, in March 2020 after the Italian prime minister locked down the entire country. Only essential businesses such as supermarkets and pharmacies could remain open.

Many local politicians considered the lockdowns an overreaction and advised citizens to carry on as usual. Media reports showed bars and restaurants in Milan and other cities filled with people ignoring rules for social distancing. With schools closed, students chafed at being idle. Large numbers gathered for games and impromptu beach parties instead of observing the quarantine. In addition, old habits of hugging and social kissing persisted despite warnings to avoid close contact. Health experts feared that such casual attitudes toward the coronavirus were leading to disaster. "If this continues, we risk not being able to open the borders between regions," Francesco Boccia, Italy's minister for regional affairs, told the Italian daily *La Stampa*. "We must not forget that we are still in the COVID-19 pandemic, and those who irresponsibly celebrate nightlife are betraying the sacrifices made by millions of Italians."[14]

Other factors helped make Italy's COVID-19 situation the worst in Europe. Its population is older, on average, than that of any other European nation and second only to Japan's worldwide. Chinese health officials discovered early on that the coronavirus is especially lethal for the elderly. Death rates can run as high as 15 percent among those age eighty or older, compared to about 3.4 percent for all ages. (Death rate is calculated by dividing the number of deaths by the number of cases.) Moreover, many families in Italy live in households with multiple generations. That allowed for easy transmission of the virus from younger people to older, more vulnerable relatives. Also, air pollution in heavily populated regions, along with high rates of cigarette smoking, contributed to widespread lung disease and breathing problems. For many Italians, this increased the likelihood of a severe reaction to the coronavirus. Together, these factors compounded the threat from COVID-19.

> "If this continues, we risk not being able to open the borders between regions. We must not forget that we are still in the COVID-19 pandemic, and those who irresponsibly celebrate nightlife are betraying the sacrifices made by millions of Italians."[14]
>
> —Francesco Boccia, Italy's minister for regional affairs

A Controversial Nursing Home Policy

On March 25, near the height of the COVID-19 outbreak in New York, Governor Andrew Cuomo introduced a controversial policy for nursing homes and long-term care facilities. Cuomo ordered these facilities to accept or readmit coronavirus patients from hospitals. The patients were not required to be tested before being readmitted. Critics charge that the policy allowed still-contagious patients to infect others in the homes. They believe the policy led to thousands of unnecessary deaths. More than twenty-three hundred residents of nursing homes and assisted care facilities in New York had died from COVID-19 by early May 2020. A report by the New York State Department of Health added twenty-five hundred more deaths to the total. The new policy was withdrawn on May 10.

Cuomo said the policy sought to prevent discrimination against the elderly. It kept nursing homes from rejecting patients due to lack of staff or protective equipment. The state health commissioner supported Cuomo's defense of the policy. However, some advocates for the elderly hoped for better policies going forward. "Obviously the way it rolled out here was pretty disastrous for people," says Richard J. Mollot, head of the Long Term Care Community Coalition, "for residents and their families."

Quoted in Shannon Young, "Cuomo Under Fire for Response to Covid-19 at Nursing Homes," Politico, May 7, 2020. www.politico.com.

Overwhelming the Health Care System

Despite the challenges, officials in Lombardy felt secure that its hospitals and emergency personnel could handle the influx of COVID-19 patients. The Lombardy health care system was ranked among the finest in Europe. However, most spending went toward clinics that delivered profitable services for wealthy patients. Emergency services, care for the elderly, and general care—the most vital areas for treating COVID-19 patients—had been neglected.

As the coronavirus spread, hospitals all over Lombardy rapidly became overwhelmed. Each day brought a deluge of new patients, many of them already in the grip of pneumonia and finding it difficult to breathe. Doctors and aides scrambled to provide treatment while also trying to protect themselves from infection. Throughout the Lombardy region, twelve out of every one hundred coronavirus cases were health care workers. Administrators soon reported shortages of masks, gloves, gowns, protective gear, respirators, and other equipment. Most serious was the shortage in hospital beds. A widely shared video showed a hospital in Bergamo where an emergency ward had been converted to an intensive care unit (ICU) because the regular ICU was full. Such scenes played out across northern Italy. Doctors of all descriptions—including surgeons, orthopedists, and cancer specialists—were enlisted to treat patients who were moaning and gasping for air.

As the crisis grew worse, doctors faced terrible choices of who would receive treatment. With facilities jammed to overcapacity, it was decided that treatment should favor younger patients with better chances of survival instead of very old patients who would require days of intensive care. Those with preconditions such as diabetes and heart disease also were deemed lower priority. This sort of triage—separating out patients by different levels of urgency—is usually reserved for the battlefield, not a suburban hospital. Medical staff wiped tears from their eyes at the appalling necessity of abandoning the desperately ill. "We decide based on age, and on health conditions," said Christian Salaroli, a physician in Bergamo, "just like all war situations."[15]

By March 21, 2020, Italy had recorded forty-eight hundred deaths from COVID-19, at that time the highest official toll in the world. In Lombardy, where piles of bodies had to be stored in churches, the government sent in troops to enforce the lockdown. With factories closed, parks shut down, and even long walks and runs banned, Italy maintained some of the toughest antivirus measures in Europe. Yet the brutal days of March gave way to better numbers in April and May. By July there were few new cases to report, even in the hard-hit Northwest. Italy had gone from global outcast to a surprising example of success against the coronavirus.

Panic and Paranoia in Iran

Another cautionary tale about the virus played out in Iran. The first deaths from COVID-19 occurred in the holy city of Qom on February 19. Over the next two months, panic arose among Iranian citizens over the worst outbreak in the Middle East. Economic sanctions imposed by the United States limited Iran's means to import medicines and equipment to address the crisis. Although the government did create and staff more than twelve hundred testing centers to screen people for infection, it failed to stress social distancing and downplayed the threat in various ways. Shrines in Qom that attracted thousands of pilgrims from inside and outside Iran were left open for weeks after the first outbreak. On February 25 President Hassan Rouhani referred to the novel coronavirus as "one of the enemy's plots to bring our country into closure by spreading panic."[16] By March 17 Iran had amassed more than 16,000 cases and 988 deaths.

Fearing a spillover of the pandemic from Iran, neighboring countries urged the United States to ease the sanctions for temporary relief. The United States refused but instead offered humanitarian packages of supplies and medicines. Rouhani declined the offer, as well as an aid mission from the international medical group Doctors Without Borders. While Iranian scientists have developed several promising therapies for COVID-19, including an antibody-rich blood treatment, Iran has also fallen victim to fake medicines. For example, hundreds of Iranians were killed or blinded by drinking bootleg methanol as a COVID cure. Too often in Iran, medical science was overruled by superstition, paranoia, and conspiracy theories.

The World's Worst Hot Spot

Health experts in the United States did not deny the existence of the novel coronavirus, but few could foresee the coming onslaught. The Trump administration had set travel restrictions to and from China that took effect on February 2, 2020. However, health officials at first tended to minimize the threat. New York City health commissioner Oxiris Barbot dismissed fears about the novel coronavirus in early February when she urged New Yorkers

An Iranian cleric and relatives of a man who died from COVID-19 pray over his body in the holy city of Qom in March 2020. Iran experienced one of the worst outbreaks of the novel coronavirus in the Middle East.

to gather for a Lunar New Year parade and street festival in Chinatown. In late February Dr. Anthony Fauci, who would become America's most trusted source for information about the coronavirus, declared that the risk was still low, although he admitted that could change. At a White House meeting on February 27, Trump said of the coronavirus, "It's going to disappear. One day it's like a miracle, it will disappear."[17] Many media outlets also downplayed the risk, assuring people that COVID-19 was less of a concern than the seasonal flu.

On February 29 a patient near Seattle, Washington, became the first COVID-19 fatality in the United States. Experts believe the coronavirus likely had been circulating on the West Coast much earlier. As the virus reached American shores, testing for infections in the United States lagged from the start. The Centers for Disease Control and Prevention (CDC) failed in its first attempt to produce an accurate diagnostic test. Moreover, there were shortages of materials for testing, including nasal swabs and reagents. At a time when testing needed to ramp up quickly to trace the coronavirus's path, health officials scrambled to establish effective protocols.

A flurry of cases in long-term care facilities in Washington State raised fears that the virus was on the move. Yet the most severe outbreak in the United States—and in the world—struck like a hammer blow in New York City. Conditions in the city helped increase the spread of the novel coronavirus. New York City's 8.3 million residents live closely packed in a confined area. On average there are twenty-seven thousand people per square mile, three times the density of Los Angeles. New Yorkers squeeze together on subways, pile into restaurants and bars, and brush past each other hourly on crowded sidewalks. Also, the city's outer boroughs, including Brooklyn and Queens, share aspects with Italy that made the pandemic more deadly. Many extended families share small apartments in which older relatives are more likely to catch the virus. Conditions such as diabetes and high blood pressure, along with obesity, plague many residents and make them more susceptible to serious reactions to COVID. As a result, new cases multiplied, then began to explode at an alarming rate. New York City rapidly became the world's worst hot spot for COVID-19.

Flattening the Curve in New York

Health officials in New York realized that a catastrophe was brewing. They were desperate to avoid the COVID-19 disaster in Italy, where hospitals were overwhelmed with patients and had to make agonizing decisions about who should receive care. On March 20 Governor Andrew Cuomo instituted a strict lockdown policy in New York that required all nonessential businesses to close. He urged New Yorkers not to venture out except to buy food, medicine, and necessary supplies. The idea of the lockdown was to "flatten the curve"—meaning to reduce the sudden steep rise in coronavirus cases as shown on a graph. If cases increased more slowly, then there would be adequate numbers of hospital beds and ICU setups to handle the influx of seriously ill patients.

The delayed lockdown, however, could not prevent a startling surge of COVID patients in New York City. By March 26, out of seventy-four thousand coronavirus cases in the United States, half were in New York—which was nearly ten times more than any other state. As in Italy's Lombardy region, New York City's beleaguered hospitals and clinics resembled a war zone. Doctors and medical personnel pleaded for more protective gear and equipment. State health officials declared a need for thirty thousand to forty thousand more ventilators to help patients who could barely breathe on their own. Many hospitals converted unused floors to makeshift ICUs to accommodate the overflow. Brookdale University Hospital Medical Center in Brooklyn experienced some of the worst challenges. Its ICUs were full, and patients' beds were parked randomly in emergency department hallways. Many of the patients were African American or Hispanic, with other health problems and a history of inadequate care. Overworked medical staff did their best to ease the patients' suffering and anxiety. "A medical war zone," Dr. Arabia Mollette described her emergency room. "Every day I come, what I see on a daily basis, is pain, despair, suffering and health care disparities."[18]

> "[It's] a medical war zone. Every day I come, what I see on a daily basis, is pain, despair, suffering and health care disparities."[18]
>
> —Arabia Mollette, an emergency physician at Brooklyn's Brookdale University Hospital Medical Center

Before the onslaught began to level off in late June, New York had lost more than thirty-one thousand lives to COVID-19. New York City alone had seen twenty-two thousand COVID fatalities. The neighboring state of New Jersey, facing a similar challenge, had lost another fifteen thousand. These were the hardest-hit areas in the world so far.

From the early example of the *Diamond Princess* in quarantine to the besieged hospitals of Lombardy and New York City, COVID-19 not only spread illness and death but also widespread feelings of panic and helplessness. Policies of lockdown, testing, and social distancing slowed the virus's spread but could not eliminate the threat. And medical experts warned that the pandemic was still far from over.

CHAPTER THREE

Successes and Struggles in Controlling the Spread

In late February 2020 it looked as though South Korea was facing a disastrous outbreak of the novel coronavirus, perhaps among the worst in the world. Health officials traced a deadly cluster of new infections to a woman belonging to a religious group in the city of Daegu. Hundreds of new infections were being reported each day, with a high of 909 cases on February 29. But the South Korean government sprang into action, determined to tackle the problem aggressively.

Medical personnel fanned out to conduct contact tracing. Anyone who might have been infected by those with the virus were placed in quarantine. In addition, the government set up testing centers across the nation. The rapid, targeted response served to bring the spiraling number of cases under control. All this was accomplished without closing down bars, restaurants, or movie theaters. On April 15, 29 million South Koreans were able to vote in a national election, with no associated new cases. Voters wore masks and gloves and had their temperatures taken before entering polling places. It was evidence that COVID-19 could be corralled with intelligence, vigor, and public trust. "The greatest leverage we have for controlling COVID-19 is people's trust in the state," says health and welfare minister Park Neung-hoo. "For this, it is very important to provide relevant information to the people in the most transparent possible manner."[19]

Better Data and More Transparency

Besides public cooperation, South Korea had experience with another dangerous virus to draw upon. Health officials had learned important lessons from dealing with Middle East respiratory syndrome, or MERS, in 2015. In that outbreak, officials failed to keep track of who was infected and which hospitals had admitted them. Government policy sought to shield patients' privacy as well as protect hospitals from public fears of contamination. But as the MERS outbreak became more widespread, many South

Voters cast their ballots at a polling station in Seoul, South Korea, in the national election on April 15, 2020. Voters had their temperatures taken before entering polling places, and there were no new cases associated with the election.

Koreans called for greater transparency. This enabled the government to pass a major new law, the Infectious Disease Control and Prevention Act. It became legal for authorities to gather, use, and make public certain personal information during an outbreak of infectious disease.

When the COVID-19 virus spread from Wuhan in January 2020, South Korea set up a round-the-clock emergency response system to screen all travelers arriving from that city. One station for monitoring fever stopped a woman at Incheon Airport before she could board a flight for Japan. Instead, she was transferred to a hospital an hour away in Seoul, where she spent fourteen days in quarantine. Health officials were also able to track the movements of those infected with great precision, using data from smartphone carriers and credit card companies. Those who had likely been exposed were notified and urged to self-quarantine. Data about hospital admittance and patient numbers were carefully compiled and sifted for trends. Citizens approved of these steps as necessary to protect public health. For most South Koreans, the need to suppress the coronavirus overrode most concerns about violations of privacy. A March 4 poll taken by the Seoul National University Graduate School of Public Health found that 78 percent of one thousand people agreed that government efforts to trace and contain COVID-19 outweighed protections of privacy rights.

The Benefits of Rapid Testing

Another important lesson was the need for rapid testing. Tests for MERS had been cumbersome and took days to get results. With COVID-19, authorities wasted no time authorizing a new test for the coronavirus. "In mid-January, our health authorities quickly conferred with the research institutions here [to develop a test]," says Kang Kyung-wha, South Korea's foreign minister. "And then they shared that result with the pharmaceutical companies, who then produced the reagent [chemical] and the equipment needed for the testing."[20] By February 26 South Korea had already tested 46,127 cases—at a time when the United States had yet to test 500.

South Africa's Remarkable Anti-COVID Success

As one of the world's most unequal societies, South Africa seemed certain to be ravaged by the novel coronavirus. The richest cities in South Africa also contain huge pockets of people struggling with poverty. When South Africa's wealthy travelers brought the coronavirus home with them in March 2020, international aid groups feared a disaster in the making. The virus spread rapidly at first, with cases more than tripling within five days in late March. Lower-income South Africans who depend on public transportation, live in large households, and reside in crowded neighborhoods faced a likely fate of disproportionate losses. In addition, large numbers have chronic health problems, such as diabetes and respiratory illness.

However, South Africa has become a success story in confronting COVID-19. Lockdowns in the nation came early and were especially aggressive. The government emphasized mask wearing and distributed oxygen supplies where needed for the seriously ill. Overall, South Africa's death rate has been seven times lower than Great Britain's. Experts attribute much of this success to the nation's youthful population. "Age is the highest risk factor [for COVID-19]," says Tim Bromfield, a regional director for the Tony Blair Institute for Global Change. "Africa's young population protects it."

Quoted in Andrew Harding, "Coronavirus in South Africa: Scientists Explore Surprise Theory for Low Death Rate," BBC, September 2, 2020. www.bbc.com.

Drive-through testing centers made it easy for people to determine, without delay, whether they had contracted the virus. Workers in protective suits administered the tests while patients remained in their cars. For subway users and nondrivers, the government also provided walk-in testing clinics the size of phone booths. Medical personnel could take a patient's nose and mouth swabs in less than a minute. The workers conducted the tests with rubber gloves embedded in clear glass walls, much like a biosafety lab. After each test, the booth was disinfected and the glass walls wiped down. The speed and convenience of the

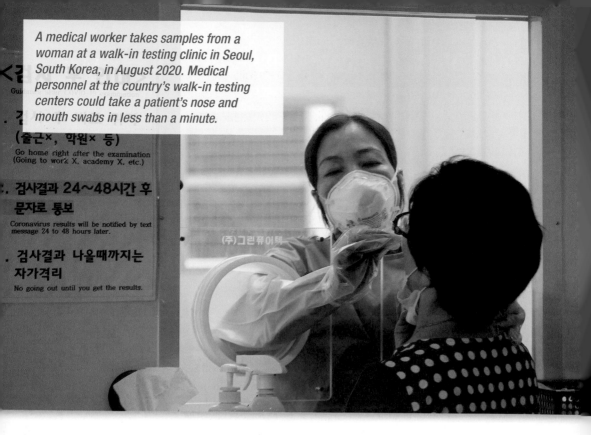

A medical worker takes samples from a woman at a walk-in testing clinic in Seoul, South Korea, in August 2020. Medical personnel at the country's walk-in testing centers could take a patient's nose and mouth swabs in less than a minute.

testing process made South Koreans more likely to get tested. The number of tests tripled in many areas. Such widespread testing produced a higher number of positive cases but did not lead to panic, because the public was reassured that serious antivirus measures were being employed.

South Koreans also have followed government advice to wear masks and gloves and to practice social distancing. Many citizens began taking these precautions even before receiving official guidelines. National and local governments were able to share data and collaborate on antivirus strategies from the beginning. As a result, on April 30 there were only four new cases in the whole country. All were travelers arriving from outside South Korea. It was the first day in two and a half months without a single local infection. As the government relaxed some of its guidelines, case numbers began to creep up again by June. However, medical experts in South Korea take pride in their nation's overall success against the novel coronavirus. "I think that early patient detection with accurate tests followed by isolation can lower the mortality rate and prevent the virus from spreading," says Professor Gye Cheol Kwon, chair of South Korea's Laboratory Medicine Foundation. "To learn from the past and prepare systems in advance . . . that might be the true power to overcome this new kind of disaster."[21]

Japan's Curious Success

Along with South Korea, Hong Kong and Singapore managed to suppress the novel coronavirus with aggressive early testing. As of mid-September 2020, South Korea had recorded only 363 deaths, Hong Kong only 100 deaths, and Singapore only 27. Other South Asian nations had similar success with strong measures. Malaysia had reported only 127 deaths, and Macau none at all. However, these positive results did not come without a cost. In Malaysia, for example, lockdowns and an economic slump hit the poorest families very hard. "The change in diet was quite shocking," says Muhammad Abdul Khalid, managing director of DM Analytics, a Malaysian consulting firm that published a study of the country's poor for the United Nations. "Egg consumption skyrocketed as one of the cheapest proteins. Rice went up 40 per cent, as did noodles. . . . We can already predict issues of malnutrition. One in three kids already face malnutrition, and with schools shuttered many children were not even able to access government-funded breakfasts."[22]

> "The change in diet [for Malaysia's poor] was quite shocking. . . . One in three kids already face malnutrition, and with schools shuttered many children were not even able to access government-funded breakfasts."[22]
>
> —Muhammad Abdul Khalid, managing director of DM Analytics

Another populous Asian nation managed to achieve a curious success against the coronavirus. Japan, with its huge, densely packed cities and the world's largest elderly population per capita, would seem to be especially vulnerable to a serious outbreak. Yet Japanese officials have responded to COVID-19 by going against conventional wisdom in almost every way. In February, as the rest of the world raised barriers to Chinese travelers, especially those from Wuhan, Japan kept its borders open. Although the government declared a state of emergency in early April, it never ordered a mandatory lockdown as most of Europe did. Instead, Japanese citizens were urged to stay home and practice social distancing. Nonessential businesses were not required to close but were asked to do so, with no penalty if they refused. Moreover, Japan mostly ignored the WHO's urgent advice to do widespread testing. By early July health officials had tested just 0.27 percent of the population, or about 350,000. In five months Japan reported only about 20,000 confirmed cases, with fewer than 1,000 deaths. And random testing for antibodies has shown very low levels of exposure among Tokyo's 37 million residents. As of September 2020 the city had suffered only 382 deaths from COVID-19.

Japan's surprising success with the coronavirus has puzzled medical experts. Some believe the Japanese—and indeed Asians throughout the region—have developed a special immunity due to prior bouts with SARS-like respiratory illness. Others credit Japan's more practical responses. Since the 1950s, when Japan was fighting outbreaks of tuberculosis, it has maintained a nationwide network of health centers to track and trace new infections. Teams of specialists are sent to areas suspected of harboring a new outbreak. Also, the Japanese regularly wear masks in public, even if only troubled with the sniffles. "I think [a mask] acts as a physical barrier," says Keiji Fukuda, an influenza specialist and director of the School of Public Health at Hong Kong University. "But it also serves as a reminder to everybody to be mindful. That we still have to be careful around each other."[23]

> "I think [a mask] acts as a physical barrier. But it also serves as a reminder to everybody to be mindful. That we still have to be careful around each other."[23]
>
> —Keiji Fukuda, director of Hong Kong University's School of Public Health

Battling Waves of Cases in India

Dr. Santhosh Kumar, an infectious disease specialist in India, often feels overwhelmed in his efforts to battle COVID-19. His nation of 1.3 billion people, four times more populous than the United States, is on pace to register the most coronavirus infections in the world. And although the total number of deaths in India is still far below the totals in the United States and Brazil, in the late summer of 2020 it reported the world's highest number of daily deaths. Kumar's fear is that India's fragile health care system will soon be swamped.

Kumar has assembled an army of health care workers and volunteers to help him confront new waves of the disease in southern India. His volunteers help fill the gaps in emergency care where needed. In outbreak areas, he and members of his team can convert unused hospital space into emergency wards in record time. Once the makeshift ICUs are operational, the overflow patients can be treated and space made for new cases. "We want to get our patients well as soon as possible, to try to create more beds," says Kumar. "How long this will last is extraordinarily hard to figure out. It's a test of our endurance."

Quoted in Vibhuti Agarwal, "For Doctor in India, Coronavirus Waves Just Keep Coming," *Wall Street Journal*, September 13, 2020. www.wsj.com.

Missteps and Protests

Not all Asian nations met with Japan's success. Some stumbled due to inadequate responses. In Indonesia, where the rate of testing was among the world's lowest and contact tracing was rare, infections soared. In mid-September 2020 Indonesia's death toll from COVID-19 stood at more than eighty-eight hundred, which was the highest total in Southeast Asia. Experts suspect that Indonesia's true number of COVID deaths is nearly three times higher. And the worst may lie ahead. "Our concern is that we have not reached the peak yet, that the peak may come around October and may not finish this year," says Iwan Ariawan, an epidemiologist from the University of Indonesia. "Right now we can't say it is under control."[24] In late August, Indonesia announced it was barring tourists until a vaccine becomes available.

The Philippines also has struggled to suppress the coronavirus, as the number of cases and deaths have spiked in that nation. The Philippines' strict lockdown in April brought economic hardship but failed to slow the spread of COVID-19. Filipinos have protested what many see as the government's missteps on policy, such as health secretary Francisco Duque's statement that healthy people need not wear masks in public. They also have charged the government with failure to protect medical personnel on the front lines of the virus battle. In September the Philippines cut the social distancing minimum on crowded public transport to 12 inches (30 cm). This was one-third of the previous requirement. Medical experts predicted that the new rules would only increase risks of infection among Filipinos. "This will be risky, reckless and counter-intuitive and will delay the flattening of the curve," says Anthony Leachon, ex-president of the Philippine College of Physicians. "Even if you wear a face shield and mask, reducing the distance between, it will be dangerous."[25] The nation saw its overall number of cases double in little over a month and, on September 14, also broke its one-day record for deaths with 259.

Controversy in Sweden

One of the world's most controversial coronavirus policies was adopted in Sweden. Unlike most European countries, the Swedish government never imposed a compulsory lockdown. Instead, it relied on voluntary actions by its citizens. One of the nation's few legal bans forbade gatherings of more than fifty people. Otherwise, Swedes were free to visit bars and restaurants, shop where they wanted, and attend theaters and other entertainments. Schools have remained open throughout the pandemic. Anders Tegnell, Sweden's chief epidemiologist, designed the plan and considers it a success. He believes it enabled the nation to weather the COVID-19 storm without wrecking the economy or disrupting the overall health care system. Tegnell also notes that trusting Swed-

People gather at a beach in Stockholm, Sweden, in August 2020. Unlike most European countries, Sweden did not impose a compulsory lockdown but instead relied on voluntary actions by its citizens during the pandemic.

ish citizens to take responsibility in controlling the virus was just as effective as a strict lockdown.

Critics strongly disagree with Tegnell. They point out that Sweden's per capita death rate is one of the highest not only in Europe but the world. These critics insist that comparisons with Sweden's neighbors—which did institute lockdowns—are telling. According to mid-August figures, while Sweden had recorded fifty-seven COVID deaths per one hundred thousand people, Denmark had logged eleven and Norway only five. Sweden's economic downturn has been less extreme than its neighbors' but only slightly.

Tegnell's response to his critics is that freedom matters. He argues that much of the disparity in death rates is owing to mistakes made in protecting elderly Swedes in nursing homes. As for the economic impact, Tegnell is adamant. "This has never been done to save the economy," he says. "It's been done to save public health."[26] By this, Tegnell means all public health, not just issues related to the coronavirus. He also notes that Sweden's number of new cases has plummeted. He believes the nation is much closer to establishing herd immunity than its neighbors. Herd immunity is when a sufficient percentage of the population has already had the virus so as to halt further spread. No doubt the debates about Sweden's coronavirus response are far from over.

Nations varied widely in their response to COVID-19. Some were quick to institute restrictions, testing, and tracing, while others hesitated, allowing the virus to spread through the population. Success stories, such as in South Korea, often turned on citizens' trust in what their government was doing to counter the pandemic. Other governments struggled to control the coronavirus's spread, often by refusing to institute lockdowns or to enforce wearing of masks and social distancing. Research on which policies were most effective against COVID-19 are likely to influence government responses in the next large pandemic.

CHAPTER FOUR

Resurgence in the United States and Elsewhere

Nancy Griffith manages a contact-tracing team for coronavirus cases in Washington County, Oregon. In March 2020, with Oregon in full lockdown, Griffith's job was fairly easy and straightforward. She and her team had to call, on average, fewer than five people for each infected patient. Griffith notes that contact numbers were low because people were not partying or exercising at the gym during the lockdown. But that all changed on June 1 when the state reopened. Bars, restaurants, shops, and gyms began to fill with customers anxious to restart their normal lives. Infected individuals generally were coming into contact with dozens of others. Each of these contacts had to be warned that they might have been infected and then advised to self-quarantine. Griffith's twenty-six team members scrambled to deliver the news within twenty-four hours to each person on their list.

The situation raised concerns that states were reopening too quickly, before enough new contact-tracing teams could be ramped up for the challenge. A simulation program developed at George Washington University estimated that the United States needs more than 218,000 contact tracers. Although estimates of the actual numbers varied, health officials feared there were far too few tracers to manage the virus's spread. Officials started to see a resurgence of the disease in many regions of the nation. "Fatigue around the virus is very real," says Griffith, "but we're at a cusp of whether this is really going [to] spiral out of control."[27]

A Summer Resurgence of COVID-19

The summer resurgence of the novel coronavirus in the United States came as many states eased lockdowns and edged back toward business as usual. Trump repeatedly urged mayors and governors to end the lockdowns in order to boost the slumping economy. The lockdowns, which were originally promoted as short-term measures to slow the virus's spread and prevent hospitals from being swamped with patients, had extended for weeks. With nonessential businesses ordered to close, millions of people lost their jobs, and many smaller enterprises like restaurants and shops went bankrupt. By April 18 more than 26 million Americans had filed for unemployment benefits. In the second quarter of the year, the economy shrank by 33 percent, sending the country into a deep recession.

Local leaders tried to balance the urge to get people working again with the responsibility to protect vulnerable populations from COVID-19. Not only health officials but also many economists saw the health care issue as more urgent. Just as the virus was exploding into a crisis in late March, Jerome H. Powell, chair of the Federal Reserve, stressed this idea. "The first order of business will be to get the spread of the virus under control, and then to resume economic activity," Powell said. "The virus is going to dictate the timetable here."[28] Yet despite the Trump administration's assurances that conditions were improving, neither objective was being met. As states began to reopen, the number of new cases continued to rise.

> "The first order of business will be to get the spread of the virus under control, and then to resume economic activity. The virus is going to dictate the timetable here."[28]
>
> —Jerome H. Powell, chair of the Federal Reserve

Many nonessential businesses, like this one in Somerville, Massachusetts, remained closed for weeks during the pandemic. During the lockdowns around the nation, millions of people lost their jobs, and many smaller enterprises like restaurants and shops went bankrupt.

A Chaotic, Patchwork Approach

The Trump administration's COVID-19 response was already judged a failure by many political analysts, medical experts, and a large majority of the American public. From the start Trump had taken what many saw as a chaotic, patchwork approach to managing the pandemic. Due to America's federal system and the Tenth Amendment, the president cannot order the states to take specific measures against the pandemic. Yet instead of setting out overall guidelines to be followed, the administration left most decisions to governors and mayors. As a result, policies regarding not only shutdowns but mask wearing, social distancing, and restrictions on large gatherings varied widely throughout the nation.

Diverging political views were bound to affect the battle against the coronavirus. In general, left-leaning states opted for more restrictive policies, with longer and more comprehensive lockdowns, while conservative states chose the opposite. Yet time and again Trump undermined calls for unity. One day the president would pledge to work with governors who had instituted strict lockdowns; the next he would tweet his support for protests against the lockdowns. Through it all, the country remained divided and uncertain. "The failure is national," wrote the *Atlantic*'s George Packer. "And it should force a question that most Americans have never had to ask: Do we trust our leaders and one another enough to summon a collective response to a mortal threat? Are we still capable of self-government?"[29]

Early in the pandemic, when governors had pleaded for help in obtaining masks, gowns, gloves, ventilators, and other essential equipment, Trump had advised them to do it themselves. The chief financial officer of the largest health care system in central Massachusetts used his own credit card to purchase $100,000 worth of N95 surgical masks, knowing that the federal government would not provide the masks in time. State health officials and hospital administrators described the competition for medical

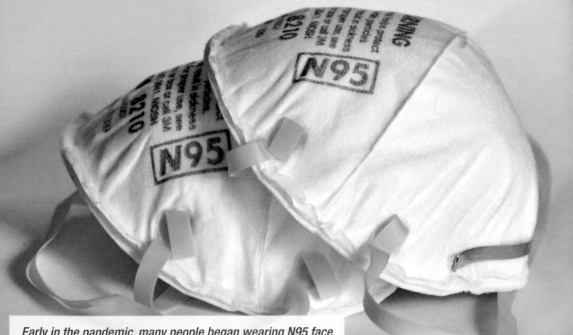

Early in the pandemic, many people began wearing N95 face masks (pictured), making this essential piece of medical equipment hard to find for health care professionals.

A Nobel-Quality Analyst

Michael Levitt, a Nobel Prize–winning biophysicist at Stanford University, has been remarkably accurate in his calculations of how the novel coronavirus would spread. Beginning in January 2020, Levitt began analyzing the rise of cases throughout the world. From his analysis, he was able to forecast trends in South Korea and other countries with great accuracy.

Levitt acknowledges much uncertainty about the coronavirus. However, his analysis has proved to be effective. He measures COVID-19 deaths in terms of excess deaths compared to the annual average. This accounts for the fact that some people who have died from COVID-19—many of whom were elderly—were likely to die over the same time from something else. Levitt estimated in April 2020 that the number of deaths associated with the coronavirus in the United States would probably be around three hundred thousand. He noted that total was likely to occur over two to three years.

In making his calculations, Levitt notes the importance of learning from details about the pandemic so that knowledge can be applied to future outbreaks. And he adds, "Our artificial intelligence is developing so quickly that maybe, in the next outbreak, we'll be able to say 'hey Siri, Alexa, Google—should I panic?'"

Quoted in Hannah Osborne, "Why the COVID-19 Death Forecasts Are Wrong," *Newsweek*, April 21, 2020. www.newsweek.com.

equipment as a free-for-all with no rules. "There was a sense," says Eric Dickson, chief executive of UMass Memorial Health Care, "that we were all alone. There was nobody coming, there was no help coming. You were going to have to manage this on your own."[30] A March survey of 213 American cities found that 91.5 percent did not have enough face masks for medical workers and first responders. More than 88 percent said they did not have sufficient personal protective equipment for medical personnel.

Problems also arose with testing for the coronavirus. Whereas South Korea's government had turned to private companies to provide an enormous number of tests rapidly in an emergency, the Trump administration relied on the CDC for early testing. However, the agency's test kits proved faulty due to contaminated chemical reagents. The government lost precious days in which cases went unidentified. By the time replacement tests were ready, the coronavirus had already spread so widely in hot spot areas that contact tracing was nearly useless. "During those early weeks, the virus took off, infecting thousands of people and leading to nationwide social distancing and sheltering in place," observes health reporter Rachana Pradhan. "Public health officials are just beginning to grapple with the fallout from that early bungling of testing, which is likely to haunt the country in the months to come."[31] Months later the government, in conjunction with private industry, had ramped up the production of testing kits to impressive levels, and the distribution of the kits to the states resulted in a total of more than 27 million tests as of June 23, 2020. But results were often unreliable or were delayed too long to be effective.

Overall, the Trump administration struggled to contain the pandemic. In August the United States ranked eighth in the world in per capita death rates, with 47.9 per 100,000. The United States had the world's highest totals of coronavirus cases and deaths. By the end of September the nation had recorded more than 7 million cases and nearly 207,000 Americans had died from COVID-19.

A Dramatic Spike in Florida

Amid an avalanche of criticism over its COVID-19 response, the Trump administration took pains to highlight success stories around the country. One of these was Florida. Despite having a larger population than New York and a huge number of elderly residents, the Sunshine State had avoided a disastrous outbreak like the ones in the Northeast. Not even an influx of college-age spring break partiers had caused much of a jump in the state's low numbers of cases and deaths. In May, as Florida emerged from a partial lockdown, Trump praised Governor Ron DeSantis for doing an excellent job.

But the coronavirus seemed to have its revenge. June saw a dramatic spike in confirmed cases, doubling the previous total in only two weeks. Patient numbers in Miami-Dade County hospitals also doubled. County officials reimposed curfews, closed the beaches, and required that masks be worn. By July 4 Florida was reporting one-fifth of all new cases for the entire country. Gyms, concert halls, restaurants, and bars, which had hailed the reopening, found themselves quickly shut down again. Restaurant owners like Michael Beltran were furious at having to break the news to their desperate employees. "I had to look them in the eye and

People walk down a street in Miami Beach, Florida, after the state emerged from its partial lockdown. By July Florida was reporting one-fifth of all new cases for the entire country, and many businesses around the state were forced to shut down again.

say 'Listen, we have to close the doors again. You did everything right, but you're not going to have a job on Wednesday,'" said Beltran. "It's demoralizing and it's soul crushing. To see restaurants used as a scapegoat here is gross, when there are so many other things that are going wrong. I can't stand it."[32]

Time magazine declared Florida's renewed shutdown the new normal. Without a vaccine available yet, cities that tried to reopen risked plunging their residents back into a coronavirus hot spot. Pundits noted that twenty other states also had to pause or reverse their plans to reopen after a significant spike in hospitalizations. Suddenly, New York and New Jersey, where new cases had slowed to a trickle, stood out for COVID-19 success.

California's Reversal and Renewed Lockdown

California also saw a positive early trend turn negative by the summer. On March 19 it became the first state to order a stay-at-home shutdown. In May case numbers were low enough for Governor Gavin Newsom to order a cautious reopening. Newsom praised Californians for having bent the curve. But Memorial Day celebrations brought an uptick in cases that soon turned into a flood. By mid-July there was an average of ninety-four hundred new cases a day, an increase of 250 percent. Newsom once more ordered the shutdown of indoor restaurants, bars, movie theaters, wineries, and other businesses in the state. Experts on infectious disease believed California had become a victim of its early success. People had assumed the coronavirus was receding and had become complacent about protocols. "You know, we opened up too soon. We didn't have the virus totally under control," says Anne Rimoin, an epidemiology professor at the University of California, Los Angeles. "People are not following the rules. They're not wearing masks. They're not social distancing. They're not doing what it is that they need to do."[33] The new outbreak prompted Newsom to mandate mask wearing statewide.

A Scourge for Minority Americans

When Teresa Bradley and her husband, Marvin, contracted the coronavirus, they suspected it came from the hospital in Grand Rapids, Michigan, where Teresa works as a nurse. Regardless of how they got infected, the Bradleys faced a special challenge with the disease. As African Americans, they were more likely to die from COVID-19 than their White neighbors.

Statistics from the CDC show that Blacks and Latinos in the United States are three times more likely to get infected with the coronavirus than Whites. They are also two times more likely to die from the disease. Black and Latino Americans more often live and work in circumstances in which they are exposed to the virus. They may live in crowded multigenerational homes, use public transportation, and have jobs with frequent public contact. They are also more likely to have health conditions that increase the risk, including obesity, diabetes, and heart problems.

The Bradleys, who are in their early sixties, shared another risk due to their ages. Nonetheless, their overall health is good, and both recovered from their bouts with the disease. Thousands of minority Americans have not been so fortunate. As Marvin says, "We're most vulnerable to this thing."

Quoted in Richard A. Oppel Jr. et al., "The Fullest Look Yet at the Racial Inequity of Coronavirus," *New York Times*, July 5, 2020. www.nytimes.com.

The surge of cases placed new strains on doctors and hospital personnel throughout the state. At Eisenhower Health in Rancho Mirage, nursing director Catherine Davis and her staff were almost exhausted from dealing with seriously ill coronavirus patients day after day. A nearby US Air Force base even sent a medical team to provide help. Davis said no one on her staff had ever experienced anything like it. "Up until this (coronavirus outbreak), on my unit we would for the most part possibly lose one patient a year," she said. "We have had 40 deaths on our unit. However, we've treated over 700 patients."[34]

As California passed a new milestone of six hundred thousand cases, the most of any state, people also worried about the economic fallout. The second lockdown brought a new wave of layoffs. In Los Angeles boarded-up businesses and "For Lease" signs could be seen all along familiar streets like Melrose Avenue and the Sunset Strip. In stadium parking lots, people lined up not for game tickets or job applications but for COVID-19 tests.

A Second Wave in Europe

As summer waned, Europe also faced a second wave of coronavirus cases. In mid-September the WHO warned that weekly cases were exceeding the numbers from the first European peak in March. In one week the region reported more than three hundred thousand new patients. Fortunately, death tallies have lagged behind these spikes in cases. Experts believe this is due to better treatments and a younger profile for patients. A majority of those testing positive were young people who showed mild symptoms or were asymptomatic. In France, for example, case numbers swelled to more than eighty-three hundred a day, but deaths averaged only a few dozen, far fewer than in the spring.

WHO regional director Hans Kluge noted that the strict lockdowns in the spring and early summer had been very effective in suppressing the coronavirus. Case numbers in June had been Europe's lowest during the pandemic. Nonetheless, most governments on the continent expressed reluctance to reinstate broad lockdowns. Officials pointed out that the earlier lockdowns had sent the region's economies into the worst tailspin since World War II, and they feared more economic carnage. Spain was rocked by Europe's largest new outbreak, with ninety-seven hundred new cases each day. More than one-fifth of its hospital beds were filled with COVID-19 patients. Despite the spike in cases, death numbers remained relatively low, and health officials in Madrid and other large cities had no plans to lock down again. Germany, which imposed only a mild shutdown in the spring, had seen some of the lowest numbers of cases and deaths in Europe. Yet Federal Minister of Health Jens Spahn said he would recommend against even that level of restriction again. As Spahn told reporters in mid-September, "This virus is here to stay and it is up to us to bring it under control and learn to live with it."[35]

Following a harrowing spring in which countries struggled to deal with COVID-19, the disease seemed to have been widely subdued. But summer brought a fierce resurgence in the United States and Europe. Lockdowns that had proved mostly effective in controlling the virus were reimposed in certain US states. But as health officials confronted a potential second wave of new cases, they began to look for less drastic means to address the threat. The world today is holding its breath awaiting the next development in the story of COVID-19.

> "This virus is here to stay and it is up to us to bring it under control and learn to live with it."[35]
>
> —Jens Spahn, German federal minister of health

Introduction: A World-Changing Virus

1. Quoted in Lauren Frias, "Dr. Fauci Gave a Blunt Assessment of How the US Is Handling the Coronavirus Pandemic: Not Great," *Business Insider*, July 10, 2020. www.businessinsider.com.
2. Quoted in Jillian Wilson, "Experts Predict What Life Will Be Like After a COVID-19 Vaccine Arrives," *Huffington Post*, August 6, 2020. www.huffpost.com.

Chapter One: From Wuhan to the World

3. Quoted in Stephanie Hegarty, "The Chinese Doctor Who Tried to Warn Others About Coronavirus," *BBC*, February 6, 2020. www.bbc.com.
4. Quoted in Associated Press, "China Delayed Releasing Coronavirus Info, Frustrating WHO," June 3, 2020. www.apnews.com.
5. Quoted in Jeremy Page et al., "How It All Started: China's Early Coronavirus Missteps," *Wall Street Journal*, March 6, 2020. www.wsj.com.
6. Quoted in William Zheng and Mimi Lau, "China's Credibility on the Line as It Tries to Dispel Fears It Will Cover Up Spread of Wuhan Virus," *South China Morning Post*, January 21, 2020. www.scmp.com.
7. University of Southampton, "Early and Combined Interventions Crucial in Tackling Covid-19 Spread in China," March 11, 2020. www.southhampton.ac.uk.
8. Quoted in Rafi Letzter, "The Coronavirus Didn't Really Start at That Wuhan 'Wet Market,'" *Live Science*, May 28, 2020. www.livescience.com.
9. Guo Jing, "Coronavirus Wuhan Diary: Living Alone in a City Gone Quiet," *BBC*, January 30, 2020. www.bbc.com.
10. Quoted in Janet Weiner, "Wuhan Lockdown Halted Spread of Coronavirus Across China," *Penn LDI*, March 22, 2020. https://ldi.upenn.edu.

Chapter Two: Growing Alarm as the Virus Spreads

11. Quoted in Doug Bock Clark, "Inside the Nightmare Voyage of the Diamond Princess," *GQ*, April 30, 2020. www.gq.com.
12. Quoted in Julian Ryall, "Panic Buying, Mistrust and Economic Woes as Japan Reels from Coronavirus Outbreak," *South China Morning Post*, February 11, 2020. www.scmp.com.
13. Quoted in Melissa Godin, "Why Is Italy's Coronavirus Outbreak So Bad?," *Time*, March 10, 2020. www.time.com.
14. Quoted in Greta Privitera, "First In, Last Out: Why Lombardy Is Still Italy's Coronavirus Hotspot," Politico, May 27, 2020. www.politico .eu.
15. Quoted in Rhea Mahbubani and Dana Varinsky, "How Italy Spiraled from a Perfectly Healthy Country to Near Collapse in 24 Days as the Coronavirus Took Hold," Business Insider, March 14, 2020. www .businessinsider.com.
16. Quoted in Richard Stone, "Iran Confronts Coronavirus Amid a 'Battle Between Science and Conspiracy Theories,'" *Science*, March 29, 2020. www.sciencemag.org.
17. Quoted in Kathryn Watson, "A Timeline of What Trump Has Said on Coronavirus," CBS News, April 3, 2020. www.cbsnews.com.
18. Quoted in Miguel Marquez and Sonia Moghe, "Inside a Brooklyn Hospital That Is Overwhelmed with Covid-19 Patients and Deaths," CNN, March 31, 2020. www.cnn.com.

Chapter Three: Successes and Struggles in Controlling the Spread

19. Quoted in Charlie Campbell, "South Korea's Health Minister on How His Country Is Beating Coronavirus Without a Lockdown," *Time*, April 30, 2020. www.time.com.
20. Quoted in Jason Beaubien, "How South Korea Reined in the Outbreak Without Shutting Everything Down," NPR, March 26, 2020. www.npr.org.
21. Quoted in Laura Bicker, "Coronavirus in South Korea: How 'Trace, Test and Treat' May Be Saving Lives," BBC, March 12, 2020. www .bbc.com.
22. Quoted in Tashny Sukumaran, "Covid-19 Forces Malaysia's Poor to Live on Instant Noodles, Abandon School: UN Study," *South China Morning Post*, August 24, 2020. www.scmp.com.

23. Quoted in Rupert Wingfield-Hayes, "Coronavirus: Japan's Mysteriously Low Virus Death Rate," BBC, July 4, 2020. www.bbc.com.

24. Quoted in Tom Allard and Kate Lamb, "An Endless First Wave: How Indonesia Failed to Control the Virus," *Japan Times*, August 20, 2020. www.japantimes.co.jp.

25. Quoted in Karen Lema, "Philippines 30cm Distancing Rule Seen as 'Reckless'; Deaths Hit Record," Reuters, September 14, 2020. https://news.yahoo.com.

26. Quoted in Michael Le Page, "Is Sweden's Coronavirus Strategy a Cautionary Tale or a Success Story?," *New Scientist*, August 13, 2020. www.newscientist.com.

Chapter Four: Resurgence in the United States and Elsewhere

27. Quoted in Deanna Paul, "Contact Tracing Isn't Keeping Up with America's Reopening," *Wall Street Journal*, July 8, 2020. www.wsj.com.

28. Quoted in Jeanna Smialek, "Fed's Powell Says U.S. Must Get Virus Under Control Before Economy Restarts," *New York Times*, March 26, 2020. www.nytimes.com.

29. George Packer, "We Are Living in a Failed State," *The Atlantic*, June 2020. www.theatlantic.com.

30. Quoted in Michael C. Bender and Rebecca Ballhaus, "'Try Getting It Yourselves': How Administration Sowed Supply Chaos," *Wall Street Journal*, September 1, 2020. www.wsj.com.

31. Rachana Pradhan, "CDC Coronavirus Testing Decision Likely to Haunt Nation for Months to Come," Kaiser Health News, March 23, 2020. www.khn.org.

32. Quoted in Vera Bergengruen, "'How Do You Do a Lockdown Backwards?' Two Months After Reopening, Florida Tries to Clamp Back Down," *Time*, July 8, 2020. www.time.com.

33. Quoted in ABC7, "California Went from Bending the Curve to a Major Coronavirus Surge. What Happened?," July 21, 2020. www.abc7.com.

34. Quoted in ABC7, "California Went from Bending the Curve to a Major Coronavirus Surge. What Happened?"

35. Quoted in Bojan Pancevski and Margherita Stancati, "Europe Shuns Lockdowns in Second Wave," *Wall Street Journal*, September 17, 2020. www.wsj.com.

Centers for Disease Control and Prevention (CDC)

www.cdc.gov/coronavirus/2019-ncov

The CDC is the nation's premier public health protection agency. The agency's website devotes significant space to coronavirus and COVID-19 facts and statistics. The site also has extensive information on who is at risk, protective measures, contact tracing, community response, schools and youth, and more.

Johns Hopkins Coronavirus Resource Center (CRC)

https://coronavirus.jhu.edu

The CRC, created and run by Johns Hopkins University & Medicine, is a continuously updated source of COVID-19 data and expert guidance. The center gathers and analyzes statistics and other information related to COVID-19 cases, testing, contact tracing, and vaccine research. The site also provides links to numerous articles from a variety of sources.

National Institute of Allergy and Infectious Diseases (NIAID)

www.niaid.nih.gov

The NIAID is one of the twenty-seven Institutes and centers that make up the National Institutes of Health. Its website includes information about coronaviruses, the public health and government response to COVID-19, and treatment guidelines. It also provides details on volunteering for prevention clinical studies.

National Institutes of Health (NIH)

www.nih.gov/coronavirus

Part of the US Department of Health and Human Services, the NIH is the largest biomedical research agency in the world. Its website provides information on development of COVID-19 vaccines, testing, and treatments as well as links to other related topics.

US Food & Drug Administration (FDA)
www.fda.gov

The FDA regulates drugs, medical devices, and other products and oversees food safety. Its website provides pandemic-related statistics and information on protective equipment, treatments, and testing. It includes an extensive section of frequently asked questions about a variety of COVID-19 topics.

World Health Organization (WHO)
www.who.int/emergencies/diseases/novel-coronavirus-2019

Working within the framework of the United Nations, the WHO directs and coordinates global health issues. Its website features rolling coronavirus updates, situation reports, travel advice, facts about preventive measures such as masks, information on how the virus spreads, and more.

Additional resources: City, county, and state public health departments

Books

Michael J. Dowling and Charles Kenney, *Leading Through a Pandemic: The Inside Story of Humanity, Innovation, and Lessons Learned During the COVID-19 Crisis*. New York: Skyhorse, 2020.

Richard Horton, *The COVID-19 Catastrophe: What's Gone Wrong and How to Stop It Happening Again*. Malden, MA: Polity, 2020.

Adam Kucharski, *The Rules of Contagion: Why Things Spread— and Why They Stop*. New York: Basic Books, 2020.

Joseph D. Lasica and Karen Jubanyik, *Beat the Coronavirus: Strategies for Staying Safe and Coping with the New Normal During the COVID-19 Pandemic*. Socialbrite, 2020. Kindle.

Debora MacKenzie, *COVID-19: The Pandemic That Never Should Have Happened and How to Stop the Next One*. New York: Hachette, 2020.

Internet Sources

Laura Bicker, "Coronavirus in South Korea: How 'Trace, Test and Treat' May Be Saving Lives," BBC, March 12, 2020. www.bbc.com.

Rhea Mahbubani and Dana Varinsky, "How Italy Spiraled from a Perfectly Healthy Country to Near Collapse in 24 Days as the Coronavirus Took Hold," *Business Insider*, March 14, 2020. www.businessinsider.com.

Jessica Migala, "How Is Coronavirus Spread? Here's What You Should (and Shouldn't) Worry About," *Health*, August 18, 2020. www.health.com.

Jeremy Page et al., "How It All Started: China's Early Coronavirus Missteps," *Wall Street Journal*, March 6, 2020. www.wsj.com.

Derek Watkins et al., "How the Virus Won," *New York Times*, June 24, 2020. www.nytimes.com.

shortages of, 28, 29, 33, 49
state officials compete for,
48–49

Rimoin, Anne, 52
Rouhani, Hassan, 30

Salaroli, Christian, 29
SARS, 10, 11, 17, 24, 40
Seoul National University
Graduate School of Public
Health, 36
Singapore, 39
South Africa, 37
South Korea, 34–35
COVID deaths in, 39
Spahn, Jens, 55
Spain, 54
Spanish flu (1918–1920), 8
spread, of COVID, 7
Straits Times (newspaper), 12
surveys
of South Koreans, on COVID
control efforts *vs.* privacy
rights, 36
of US cities on availability
of personal protective
equipment, 49
Sweden, 42–44
response to coronavirus in, 8
symptoms, 7–8

Takenaka, Fumio, 23
Tegnell, Anders, 42–44
tests/testing
problems with, in US, 31,
49–50
in South Korea, **38**
Time (magazine), 52

Trump, Donald/Trump
administration, 47, 50–51
coronavirus minimized by,
31
sets travels restrictions from
China, 30
urges governors to end
lockdowns, 46, 48

United States
COVID response left to
governors in, 47–48
COVID testing problems in,
49–50
response to coronavirus in, 8
summer resurgence of
COVID in, 46
University of Southampton, 14
US Food & Drug Administration
(FDA), 60

vaccines, 7, 8
Van Kerkhove, Maria, 11

Washington, 31–32
Wei Guixian, 15
wet market, in Wuhan, 15–16,
16
World Health Organization
(WHO), 7, 60
declares COVID a global
health emergency, 20

Xi Jinping, 11, 14

Yan, Li-Meng, 15

Zhong Nanshan, 17
Zhou Xianwang, 14